W9-BEJ-414

Saying I'm Sorry

by Laura Alden
illustrated by
Dan Siculan

70

THE CHILD'S WORLD

ELGIN, ILLINOIS 60120

Distributed by Childrens Press, 1224 West Van Buren Street,
Chicago, Illinois 60607.

Library of Congress Cataloging in Publication Data

Alden, Laura, 1955-
  Saying I'm sorry.

  (What's in a word?)
  Originally published: Elgin, Ill.: Child's World,
1982. (What does it mean?)
  Summary: Rhyming text and illustrations present a
variety of situations where an apology is required.
    1. Apologizing—Juvenile literature.   [1. Apologizing.
2. Forgiveness.   3. Conduct of life]   I. Siculan,
Dan, ill.   II. Title.   III. Series.
[BF575.A75A43   1982b]   158'.2   82-19945
ISBN 0-89565-247-1

4 5 6 7 8 9 10 11 12 R 89 88 87 86 85 84

Saying I'm Sorry

Sorry—Feeling pity for someone; feeling
bad about something you have said or done.
To say, "I'm sorry," is to express that feeling.

Saying, "I'm sorry,"
is as hard sometimes as
going to bed
when you should
or putting your blocks back.

Saying, "I'm sorry,"
is as hard sometimes as
eating all your peas
without griping
or as helping wash dishes.

Saying, "I'm sorry,"
is hard sometimes.
But you feel good
when it's said.

When you say,
"I'M SORRY,"
others know you care about them.

The leaves and I
fell in a heap
      on top of and over
      each other.

And before I thought
about how leaves fly,
      I threw some way up
      in the wind.

The leaves blew back,
all over a man
      who looked from between them
      and sighed.

"I'm sorry," I said,
brushing leaves from my head.
      Smiling,
      he went on his way.

Anne drew a picture
—carefully—
of her pet cat, Emily.
She gave it to me
to carry and keep.

I dropped it
—accidentally—
into a pothole puddle
of water and mud.
The picture was drowned.

"I'm sorry," I said.
Anne blinked away tears,
but she nodded.
She understood.

The calendar said,
"Dentist at 10."
Mom waited at the door.

"Do I have time
to brush my teeth?"
I hollered down the stairs.

"You did," Mom said.
"We're late. Come on!"

The car clock read,
"Two minutes to 10."

"I'm sorry that I'm late,"
I said.

BEING SORRY

means making things right again.

The readings, the songs, the pronouncements
  were long. And we still had a long way to go.
So we started to whisper jokes to
  each other. Sometimes it's hard to be still.

After the wedding, Mom took me aside
  and told me I should apologize
to Mrs. Hammer. She couldn't hear because
  we were making so much noise.

So Jed and I apologized. And, better yet,
  next time we'll try to be quiet.

Leaping and kicking
    sand in the air,
        we ran down the beach
            side by side.

Milton ran fast
  and out of control,
    though I tried to make him
      behave.

    Over the dunes,
      down to the shore,
        right toward some kids and
          a castle!

        SMASH! Milton crashed it.
          The kids were all mad.
            Their towering castle was
              totaled.

I called Milton back.
  I said we were sorry.
    And they let me help them
      rebuild.

"Cheater!" I yelled
when he won the game.
Of course,
I didn't mean it.

But Jared's eyes got big
and sad.
He was hurt,
and I felt bad.

Later, when we went to bed,
I whispered in the dark,
"I love you,
and I'm sorry."

"I love you, too," he said.

Sometimes,
FEELING SORRY
helps you learn from your mistakes.

Shouts, shots, and pops
came from the show
that we were not to watch.

"All right," said Mom.
"Who turned on the TV?"

I had done it,
but I looked at Jared.

"Jared," Mom said.
"You know better than that—"

"I did it," I said,
and apologized,
as I should have done.

SARDINES!

We hid in a box in the basement.

Carrie found us . . . .
    Watch it! . . . OUCH!
She stepped on me (hard!)
    and I said,
"Carrie, you are too fat for this box!
    Get out!"

She started to cry
    and it was my fault.
I won't ever do that again.

Company was coming
in an hour.
"Don't mess up the house," Dad said.

I read for awhile
but then I got bored—
and, somehow, forgot what Dad said.

When the company came,
I had finished a fort
and really messed up the room.

I looked up at Dad.
I could tell he was mad.
"Sorry," I said. "I forgot . . . ."

"I'll talk to you later," Dad said.

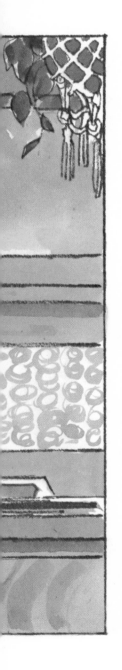

I couldn't wait
to talk to Mom,
though she was
on the phone.

I
INTERRUPTED
HER
AGAIN!

"Sorry," I said.
When <u>will</u> I learn?

25

What do you do when
OTHERS ARE SORRY?

I told them
   not to play with my train.
I told them
   to ask me first.

But they didn't ask,
   and the switch came off.
The train is down, derailed.

I told them
   not to play with it.
I told them
   to just ask.

"Sorry," they said.
   And I knew they meant it.
"It's okay," I said.

I should forgive my brother.
It's hard, though, to forgive
when you are
hurt,
or left out,
or made fun of.

But he said he was sorry.
I know how that feels.
Sometimes I'm sorry
and need forgiving.
I'll go now and say,
   "Hey, it's okay.
   Forget it."

About the Author:

Laura Alden holds a degree in communications and journalism from Bethel College (St. Paul, Minnesota). Her major professional interest and experience has been in children's publishing, in both the magazine and book fields. She is presently an editor for The Child's World, a publishing company that specializes in materials for early childhood. Ms. Alden lives in the Chicago area but thinks about Iowa a lot.

About the Artist:

Dan Siculan studied art fundamentals at the Oglebay Institute in Wheeling, West Virginia, and life drawing at the American Academy of Art in Chicago. His career began while in the army where he served as an artist while stationed in Europe. Mr. Siculan later worked as a commercial artist, becoming free lance in 1951. He is proficient in painting in oils, acrylics, and water color media and has produced numerous editions of original serigraphs. He is married and has four children and three grandchildren.